curry

curry

easy recipes for all your favorites

Sunil Vijayakar

photography by Kate Whitaker

RYLAND
PETERS
& SMALL

LONDON NEW YORK

Dedication
For Geraldine and Finn, with love.

Design and photographic art direction
Steve Painter
Senior Commissioning Editor Julia Charles
Senior Editor Céline Hughes
Production Controller Toby Marshall
Art Director Leslie Harrington
Publishing Director Alison Starling

Food Stylist Sunil Vijayakar
Prop Stylist Penny Markham
Indexer Sandra Shotter

Author's acknowledgments
Thanks to Steve for his fabulous art direction, to
Céline for her meticulous and amazing editing, to
Julia for commissioning me, to Kate for her terrific
photography, and to Belinda for assisting me.

First published in the United States
in 2008 by Ryland Peters & Small, Inc.
519 Broadway, 5th Floor
New York, NY 10012
www.rylandpeters.com

10 9 8 7 6 5 4 3 2 1

Printed in China

ISBN: 978 1 84597 726 9

Library of Congress Cataloging-in-Publication Data

Vijayakar, Sunil.
  Curry : easy recipes for all your favorites / Sunil
Vijayakar ;
photography by Kate Whitaker.
    p. cm.
  Includes index.
  ISBN 978-1-84597-726-9
1. Cookery (Curry) 2. Cookery, Southeast Asian. I.
Title.
  TX819.C9V55 2008
  641.3'384--dc22
                                    2008021861

Notes

• All spoon measurements are level, unless
otherwise specified.

• Ovens should be preheated to the specified
temperature. Recipes in this book were tested
using a regular oven. If using a convection oven,
follow the manufacturer's instructions for adjusting
temperatures.

• All eggs are medium, unless otherwise specified.
Recipes containing raw or partially cooked egg, or
raw fish or shellfish, should not be served to the very
young, very old, anyone with a compromised
immune system, or pregnant women.

• Sterilize preserving jars before use. Wash them in
hot, soapy water and rinse in boiling water. Place in
a large saucepan and then cover with hot water.
With the lid on, bring the water to a boil and
continue boiling for 15 minutes. Turn off the heat,
then leave the jars in the hot water until just before
they are to be filled. Invert the jars onto clean
kitchen paper to dry. Sterilize the lids for 5 minutes,
by boiling, or according to the manufacturer's
instructions. Jars should be filled and sealed while
they are still hot.

contents

introduction

The word "curry" is believed to originate from the south Indian Tamil word "kari," which generally describes a stew-like dish seasoned with aromatic spices and herbs. As we become increasingly global in our appreciation of food, we now know and embrace curries from all around the world, but mainly India, Pakistan, Thailand, Sri Lanka, Indonesia, Vietnam, Burma, and other Southeast Asian countries. Curries differ greatly in taste, content, texture, and flavor, each with vast regional variations and history.

Living in the West, especially in the bigger cities, we are fortunate to have such a wide variety of restaurants and eateries, due to pockets of immigrant communities that have settled here, offering authentic cuisines. There is nothing more satisfying, though, than cooking a great curry from scratch in the comfort of your own kitchen. The idea may seem daunting to the novice cook or to someone who is unfamiliar with the cuisine, but you will soon realize that cooking curries is easy, relaxing, and rewarding.

You will need a well-stocked pantry of basic ingredients and spices. Most of these can be found in any large supermarkets and with the miracle of internet shopping, you can source any exotic ingredients and have them delivered to your door (see websites & mail order, page 94). You do not need any special equipment to start cooking, just skillets or a wok, saucepans, and a food processor. Armed with your treasure trove of ingredients and spices, go ahead and enjoy cooking up the various different curries for your friends and family.

The essence of cooking curries lies in the quality of the ingredients you use, and in particular the wonderful combinations of spices, aromatics, herbs, and other flavorings that are blended and cooked to produce aromatic flavors and tastes. I urge you to browse the shelves of Asian supermarkets and specialty stores to inspire your culinary zeal and nurture your taste for the exotic. The smell of warm spices permeating the air and the piles of glorious, healthy fresh produce will be enough to have you wanting to get into your kitchen and start cooking!

ingredients

spices

Amchoor Also known as mango powder, this pale yellow powder made from dried unripe mango has a tart, fruity tang with a hint of sweetness. If unavailable, use a dash of lime or lemon juice, or tamarind water instead.

Cardamom This sweetly aromatic spice with a gingery, musky fragrance is used in sweet and savory dishes. The pods can be added to rice or split open and the seeds ground or used whole. The ground seeds are used in spice mixes such as garam masala.

Cassia Also known as Chinese cinnamon, cassia has a coarser appearance than cinnamon and a stronger flavor. If cassia is unavailable, use cinnamon instead.

Chiles Whole dried red chiles can be fiery, so use with caution. They are usually fried to enhance and intensify their flavor. Dried red pepper flakes are also available and tend to be slightly milder. Chili powders made from dried chiles are usually labeled hot, medium, or mild. Kashmiri chili powder, made from dried red Kashmiri chiles, is fiery-hot, while paprika is extremely mild, slightly sweet, and smoky.

Cinnamon This sweet, warming spice is used to flavor sweet and savory dishes. It comes from the bark of a tree related to the laurel family and is available whole or ground. Cinnamon sticks should be discarded from a dish before serving.

Cloves These very dark brown buds of an evergreen tree are pungent so they are used (whole or ground) in small quantities. Whole cloves should be discarded before serving.

Coriander The beige seeds of the coriander plant have a warm, burnt-orange aroma and are used whole or ground. To grind the seeds yourself, toast them first in a dry skillet to release the flavor.

Cumin These small, long beige seeds are used whole or ground. They have a distinctive warm, pungent aroma and are usually fried first to intensify their flavor. Whole seeds may be toasted and sprinkled over a dish before serving. To grind the seeds yourself, toast them first in a dry skillet to release the flavor.

Curry leaves These small, dark green leaves have a distinctive curry-like aroma and are found fresh in Asian stores. They freeze well. Dried leaves are not as aromatic as fresh leaves. Fresh curry leaves are usually fried first to release their flavor.

Curry powders & pastes Ready-made curry powders and pastes are an invention of the West, but are nonetheless useful pantry staples. There are many varieties, usually mild, medium, or hot, as well as specific mixes such as Madras curry powder, or tandoori spice mix. You can also get very good Thai green and red curry pastes.

Fennel These small, pale greenish-brown seeds have a subtle aniseed flavor. They are used as a flavoring or served after the meal as a digestive and breath freshener.

Fenugreek Mainly used in north Indian cooking, these tiny, yellowish seeds are used in pickles, chutneys, and vegetarian dishes.

Garam masala Every household has its own variation of this classic spice mix, which is usually added towards the end of cooking time. A classic mix contains cardamom, cloves, peppercorns, cumin, cinnamon, and nutmeg. Ready-made mixes can be bought from supermarkets and Asian stores.

Mustard seeds These are an essential flavoring in Indian cooking, particularly dals, vegetarian and rice dishes, and pickles. Black, brown, and yellow mustard seeds are usually fried until they pop to achieve a mellow, nutty flavor. The crushed, whole seeds are very peppery and are sometimes added to pickles.

Nigella Also known as black onion seeds or kalonji, these tiny, pungent black seeds are often used to flavor breads and pickles.

Peppercorns Native to the Malabar coast, these tiny, pungent berries are a very popular flavoring. They may be used whole, crushed, or freshly ground. Avoid the ready-ground spice, because it loses the fresh, pungent bite of the whole spice.

Saffron Harvested from a special crocus, these deep orange strands are used to impart a wonderfully musky fragrance to rice dishes and desserts. It is one of the most expensive spices, but only a little is needed, and it is well worth the cost. Avoid the powdered spice which is not as flavorful and may have been adulterated.

Tamarind Used as a souring agent to bring out and enhance the flavor of other ingredients, tamarind has a sharp, fruity tang. It is obtained from a pod and is usually available as a pulp, paste, or purée. The pulp needs to be soaked in hot water for several hours, then strained; the paste or purée can be dissolved in hot water.

Turmeric This bright orange-yellow rhizome has a warm, musky flavor and is used in small quantities in vegetable and lentil dishes. The fresh spice can sometimes be found in Asian stores, but it is usually easier to buy the dried, ground spice.

Urad dal A type of lentil, urad dal is used as a spice in south Indian cooking—fried first to release and intensify its nutty flavor.

wet spices & aromatics

Chiles Fresh green and red chiles are used to give heat and flavor to many curry dishes, although it should be noted that not all curries contain chiles, and many curries can be mild. Green chiles are more commonly used, although the riper red chiles feature in many dishes. Much of the heat resides in the seeds and pith so unless you want a fiery-hot dish, remove the seeds and pith before chopping the flesh.

Garlic Garlic is used with ginger and onion as the base of many classic curries. There is no substitute for the flavor of fresh garlic, which is usually sliced, crushed, or grated and fried before other spices are added.

Ginger Fresh root ginger is another essential aromatic, used in savory and sweet dishes. It has a fresh, zesty, peppery flavor; dried ground ginger is no substitute. Look for ginger with a smooth, light brown skin and peel before slicing, dicing, or grating.

Onions Onion is usually classed as a vegetable but it is such an essential flavoring (frequently used with garlic and fresh ginger), that it deserves to be placed among wet spices and aromatics.

Shallots These small, pungent members of the onion family are used in the same way as onions, and are used particularly in south Indian and south Asian cooking.

herbs

Bay leaves The whole leaves are used only occasionally in curries; the dried, ground leaves are sometimes used in garam masala.

Cilantro Fresh cilantro is an important ingredient in many savory dishes, salads, and chutneys. Its delicate leaves have a distinctive, fragrant aroma, and are usually added to dishes just before serving.

Kaffir lime leaves Highly aromatic leaves from the kaffir lime tree, usually used finely shredded or left whole. The fresh leaves freeze very well and are superior to dried.

Lemon grass This citrus-flavored "grass" is used whole by bruising the base to release the flavor, or it can be finely chopped.

Mint Fresh, zesty mint is popular in many dishes and chutneys. Although dried mint is widely available, it does not have the same zest as the fresh herb.

Thai sweet basil leaves These fragrant leaves are used to garnish many Thai and Southeast Asian-style curries.

pantry staples

Beans A good stock of dried and canned beans are essential for the pantry. Dried lentils, split peas, and pale green mung beans need no soaking and do not take long to cook, while beans such as chickpeas, black-eyed beans, and kidney beans require lengthy soaking and boiling until tender. For these types of "high-maintenance" legumes, it is worth buying the organic, canned variety to save time. Buy them packed in water, rather than brine, and rinse them well before adding to the pan.

Coconut Another essential ingredient, coconut milk and cream are added to savory dishes to add a rich sweetness and smooth, creamy texture. Although you can make your own coconut milk from fresh coconuts, it is much easier to use the canned variety, of which there are healthier low-fat versions. Desiccated coconut is also commonly used.

Gram flour Also known as besan, this golden flour made from ground chickpeas has a lovely, slightly nutty flavor and is used for thickening, binding and making batters.

Nuts & seeds These play an important role in the Indian kitchen. Ground almonds and cashew nuts are a popular addition to savory dishes, while pistachio nuts are often used to garnish savory dishes and desserts. Poppy seeds are usually toasted to intensify their taste, and used to flavor curries. White poppy seeds (khus khus) are mainly used to thicken curries.

Oils Although ghee (clarified butter) is the fat traditionally used in Indian cooking, the recipes in this book use healthier sunflower and vegetable oils. These oils have a mild flavor, so do not interfere with the subtle spicing and other flavorings of the dishes.

Rice The best rice to serve with curry is basmati. It has a fragrant aroma and light fluffy texture. It benefits from rinsing or soaking in cold water before cooking. Thai jasmine rice should be served with the green and red Thai curries.

chicken

All too often, we rely on chicken for the basis of an evening meal without really knowing how to make the best of this healthy, satisfying meat. The good news is it's perfect in a curry—and it's so versatile an ingredient that there are lots of flavors and textures that marry well with it. Imagine tender pieces of chicken thigh and succulent jumbo shrimp simmering in curried coconut milk, then spooned onto rice noodles and topped with all sorts of condiments, and you have the fabulous **Mandalay chicken noodle curry (page 15)**—a dish my good friends in Mumbai often serve up for Sunday lunch because there is so much to savor within one bowl. Meanwhile, **chicken tikka masala (page 12)** is top of Great Britain's list of favorite dishes, while **Thai green chicken curry (page 17)** is increasingly being served up in homes in the Western world for its delicate aromatics and fresh ingredients. The lesser known **Vietnamese chicken curry (page 21)** illustrates that curries needn't mean chunks of meat swimming in gravy but rather the transformation of a handful of spices into a concentrated sauce, verging on alchemy. For fuss-free suppers, **chicken & spinach curry (page 14)** and **butter chicken (page 18)** are left to marinate overnight, so that most of the work is done by the time you get round to cooking the next day.

chicken tikka masala

Boneless, marinated chicken pieces are broiled, then added to a rich, creamy, tomato-based sauce. Serve with warm Naan (page 85) or steamed basmati rice.

4 boneless, skinless chicken breasts, cut into bite-size pieces

salt and freshly ground black pepper

freshly chopped cilantro leaves, to garnish

sliced red chiles, to garnish (optional)

chicken tikka marinade

1 cup plain yogurt

1 tablespoon freshly squeezed lemon juice

2 teaspoons ground cumin

1 teaspoon ground cinnamon

2 teaspoons cayenne pepper

2 teaspoons freshly ground black pepper

1 tablespoon finely grated fresh ginger

tikka masala sauce

1 tablespoon butter

1 garlic clove, crushed

1 red chile (seeded if desired), finely chopped

2 teaspoons ground cumin

3 teaspoons paprika

7 oz canned chopped tomatoes

2 tablespoons tomato paste

¾ cup heavy cream

serves 4

To make the chicken tikka marinade, combine the yogurt, lemon juice, cumin, cinnamon, cayenne, black pepper, and ginger in a large glass bowl and season with salt. Stir in the chicken, cover, and refrigerate for 4–6 hours or overnight.

Thread the marinated chicken on to metal skewers (discarding the marinade). Cook under a hot, preheated broiler for about 5 minutes on each side.

Meanwhile, make the tikka masala sauce. Melt the butter in a large, heavy skillet over medium heat. Sauté the garlic and chile for 1 minute. Add the cumin and paprika and season well.

Purée the canned tomatoes in a blender until smooth, then add to the skillet with the cream. Simmer over low heat until sauce has thickened, about 20 minutes.

Add the broiled chicken to the skillet and simmer for 10 minutes, or until cooked through. Transfer to a serving platter and garnish with the cilantro and chiles, if using. Serve with warm naan or steamed basmati rice.

chicken & spinach curry

Serve this velvety chicken and spinach curry with steamed basmati rice and Onion, Cucumber & Tomato Relish (page 88).

To make the marinade, combine the yogurt, garlic, ginger, coriander, and curry powder in a large glass bowl and season well. Stir in the chicken, cover, and refrigerate for 3–4 hours or overnight.

Put the spinach in a saucepan and cook for 8–10 minutes. Drain thoroughly, place in a food processor, and blend until smooth. Season well.

Heat the sunflower oil in a large, nonstick skillet and add the onion. Cook over gentle heat for 10–12 minutes. Add the cumin seeds and stir-fry for 1–2 minutes.

Increase the heat to high and add the marinated chicken (discarding the marinade). Stir-fry for 6–8 minutes. Pour in the broth and spinach and bring to a boil. Reduce the heat to low, cover tightly, and cook for 25–30 minutes, or until the chicken is cooked through.

Uncover the pan, check the seasoning, and cook over high heat for 3–4 minutes, stirring often. Remove from the heat and stir in the lemon juice. Serve immediately with steamed basmati rice and Onion, Cucumber & Tomato Relish.

1¾ lb boneless, skinless chicken thighs, cut into bite-size pieces
1 lb frozen spinach, thawed
2 tablespoons sunflower oil
1 onion, finely chopped
2 teaspoons cumin seeds
⅔ cup chicken broth
1 tablespoon freshly squeezed lemon juice
salt and freshly ground black pepper

marinade
½ cup plain yogurt
2 tablespoons crushed garlic
2 tablespoons finely grated fresh ginger
2 tablespoons ground coriander
2 tablespoons medium curry powder

serves 4

Mandalay chicken noodle curry

Also known as 'khow sway', this delicious Burmese curry is the perfect choice for relaxed entertaining. If you can't find Burmese shrimp paste in the supermarket, use 1 tablespoon dark soy sauce instead.

1¾ lb boneless, skinless chicken thighs, cut into bite-size pieces

2 large onions, roughly chopped

5 garlic cloves, roughly chopped

1 teaspoon finely grated fresh ginger

2 tablespoons sunflower oil

½ teaspoon Burmese shrimp paste (belacan)

14 oz canned coconut milk

2 tablespoons medium curry powder

6½ oz raw jumbo shrimp, shelled and deveined

6½ oz rice vermicelli

salt and freshly ground black pepper

to garnish

chopped cilantro leaves

finely chopped red onion

fried garlic slivers

sliced red chiles

lime wedges

serves 4

Season the chicken and set aside.

Put the onions, garlic, and ginger in a food processor and process until smooth (you might need to add a couple of tablespoons of water).

Heat the sunflower oil in a large saucepan. Add the onion mixture and shrimp paste and cook over high heat, stirring, for about 5 minutes.

Add the chicken and cook over medium heat, stirring, until it browns. Add the coconut milk and curry powder and bring to a boil. Reduce the heat, cover, and simmer for about 40 minutes. Stir occasionally.

Stir in the shrimp and cook, uncovered, for 6–8 minutes, or until pink and cooked through.

Put the noodles in a bowl, cover with boiling water, and leave for 10 minutes. Drain and divide between 4 large, warmed bowls. Ladle the curry over the top and garnish with the cilantro, red onion, garlic, chiles, and lime wedges.

Thai green chicken curry

Pea eggplants are available from good Asian supermarkets. If you can't get hold of them, substitute with regular eggplant, cut into bite-size pieces. Serve with steamed Thai jasmine rice.

Heat the sunflower oil in a large nonstick wok or saucepan and add the curry paste and chiles. Stir-fry for 2–3 minutes, then add the chicken. Stir and cook for 5–6 minutes, or until the chicken is sealed and lightly browned.

Stir in the coconut milk, broth, lime leaves, fish sauce, palm sugar, and pea eggplants. Simmer, uncovered, for 10–15 minutes, stirring occasionally.

Add the green beans and bamboo shoots and continue to simmer for 6–8 minutes.

Remove from the heat and stir in the basil, cilantro, and lime juice. Serve with steamed Thai jasmine rice.

1 tablespoon sunflower oil

3 tablespoons Thai green curry paste

2 green chiles, finely chopped

1¾ lb boneless, skinless chicken thighs, cut into bite-size pieces

14 oz canned coconut milk

¾ cup chicken broth

6 kaffir lime leaves

2 tablespoons fish sauce

1 tablespoon grated palm sugar

6 oz pea eggplants

3 oz green beans, halved

2 oz canned sliced bamboo shoots, drained and rinsed

a large handful of fresh Thai sweet basil leaves

a large handful of cilantro leaves

freshly squeezed juice of 1 lime

serves 4

butter chicken

This popular chicken curry, natively called "makhani" has its origins in the Mughal dynasty. It is rich and irresistible. Serve with steamed basmati rice or warm Naan (page 85).

To make the marinade, heat a nonstick skillet and toast the cashew nuts, fennel seeds, cinnamon, coriander, cardamom seeds, peppercorns, and cloves for 2–3 minutes, or until very aromatic. Transfer to a spice grinder and grind until smooth.

Add this mixture to a blender with the garlic, ginger, vinegar, tomato paste, and half the yogurt and process until smooth. Transfer to a large glass bowl with the remaining yogurt. Stir in the chicken, cover, and refrigerate for 24 hours.

Melt the butter in a large, nonstick wok or saucepan and add the onion, cassia bark, and cardamom pods. Stir-fry over medium heat for 6–8 minutes, or until the onion has softened. Add the marinated chicken (discarding the marinade) and cook, stirring, for 10 minutes. Season.

Stir in the chili powder, canned tomatoes, and broth, bring to a boil, then reduce the heat to low. Simmer, uncovered, for 40–45 minutes, stirring occasionally.

Add the cream and cook gently for a further 4–5 minutes. Garnish with the cilantro and serve immediately with steamed basmati rice or naan.

1¾ lb boneless, skinless chicken thighs, cut into large bite-size pieces

3 tablespoons butter

1 large onion, finely chopped

1 cassia bark or cinnamon stick

4 cardamom pods

1 teaspoon mild or medium chili powder

14 oz canned chopped tomatoes

¾ cup chicken broth

½ cup light cream

salt and freshly ground black pepper

freshly chopped cilantro, to garnish

marinade

1 cup cashew nuts

1 tablespoon fennel seeds

2 teaspoons ground cinnamon

1 tablespoon ground coriander

1 teaspoon cardamom seeds, crushed

1 teaspoon black peppercorns

½ teaspoon ground cloves

4 garlic cloves, crushed

2 teaspoons finely grated fresh ginger

2 tablespoons white wine vinegar

6 tablespoons tomato paste

⅔ cup plain yogurt

serves 4

Vietnamese chicken curry

Even though Vietnam was colonized by the French, the traditional cuisine has more in common with their Chinese neighbors. Ground bean sauce is available in good Asian supermarkets but if you can't find it, substitute oyster sauce instead.

3 tablespoons sunflower oil

1¾ lb skinless chicken breasts, cut into thin strips

12 scallions, cut into 1-inch lengths

4 garlic cloves, finely chopped

1 red chile, thinly sliced

2 star anise

¼ cup very finely chopped lemon grass

1 teaspoon cardamom seeds, crushed

1 cinnamon stick

10 oz green beans, halved

1 carrot, cut into batons

2 tablespoons fish sauce

2 tablespoons ground bean sauce

a small handful of cilantro leaves, chopped

a small handful of fresh mint leaves, chopped

chopped roasted peanuts, to serve

serves 4

Heat half the sunflower oil in a large, nonstick skillet and stir-fry the chicken, in batches, for 1–2 minutes. Remove with a slotted spoon and keep warm.

Heat the remaining oil in the same skillet and stir-fry the scallions for 1–2 minutes, or until softened. Add the garlic, chile, star anise, lemon grass, cardamom seeds, cinnamon, green beans, and carrots. Stir-fry for 6–8 minutes.

Return the chicken to the pan with the fish sauce and ground bean sauce. Stir-fry for 3–4 minutes, or until the chicken is cooked through. Remove from the heat and sprinkle over the cilantro, mint, and peanuts before serving.

meat

For gutsy stews which take their time on the stovetop to produce deep flavors and melt-in-the-mouth lamb, beef, or pork, meat curries are second to none. Every region of India excels in its own version which has been shaped by many different influences. **Vindaloo (page 34)** hails from Goa, once colonized by the Portuguese who brought with them a pork stew from which the Indian vindaloo was born. This, along with others like **beef madras (page 33)**, is often erroneously touted as fierce and fiery, but you can adjust the heat to suit your tastes—from seeding the chiles to lessen their heat, to using mild chili powder. It's good to know that curries are flexible in this way, and it is often the case that the meats used are interchangeable too. So the **kofta curry (page 27)** and even the **lamb korma (page 29)** offer a choice of meat. A word of advice: many meat curries, particularly the **lamb rogan josh (page 24)** taste even better the day after they are made, so if you can resist the temptation to eat the whole lot in one sitting, you will really notice when the spices have melded the next day. If you're entertaining, there's a meat dish for every occasion. **Kashmiri lamb kabobs (page 28)** are ideal for a barbecue, while the **ground beef & pea curry (page 30)** is left to simmer for over an hour leaving you free to enjoy your guests' company.

lamb rogan josh

This slow-cooked lamb stew from Kashmir in north India is perfect for hassle-free entertaining as it almost cooks itself!

Heat half the sunflower oil in a large, heavy-based casserole dish and cook the lamb, in batches, for 3–4 minutes, until evenly browned. Remove with a slotted spoon and set aside.

Add the remaining oil to the dish and add the onions. Cook over medium heat for 10–12 minutes, stirring often, until soft and lightly browned.

Add the garlic, ginger, cassia, chili powder, paprika, and cardamom pods. Stir-fry for 1–2 minutes, then add the curry paste and lamb. Stir-fry for 2–3 minutes, then stir in the canned tomatoes, tomato paste, sugar, stock, and potatoes. Season well and bring to a boil. Reduce the heat to very low (using a heat diffuser if possible) and cover tightly. Simmer gently for 2–2½ hours, or until the lamb is meltingly tender.

Remove from the heat and garnish with the cilantro and a drizzle of yogurt.

2 tablespoons sunflower oil

1¾ lb boneless lamb shoulder, cut into large bite-size pieces

2 large onions, thickly sliced

3 garlic cloves, crushed

2 teaspoons finely grated fresh ginger

2 cassia barks or cinnamon sticks

2 teaspoons Kashmiri chili powder

2 teaspoons paprika

6 cardamom pods

4 tablespoons medium curry paste

14 oz canned chopped tomatoes

6 tablespoons tomato paste

1 teaspoon sugar

1⅔ cups lamb broth

4–6 potatoes, peeled and left whole

freshly chopped cilantro leaves, to garnish

whisked plain yogurt, to drizzle

serves 4

kofta curry

Every country seems to have their own version of the "kofta" or meatball. Here the meatballs are cooked in a spicy tomato sauce that is perfect served with warm Naan (page 85) or steamed basmati rice.

To make the koftas, put the ginger, garlic, cinnamon, cilantro, and mince in a mixing bowl. Season well and, using your fingers, mix well to combine. Roll tablespoons of the mixture into bite-size balls, place on a tray, cover, and chill for 1–2 hours.

Heat 2 tablespoons of the sunflower oil in a large, nonstick skillet, then add the koftas and cook in batches until lightly browned. Remove with a slotted spoon and set aside.

Add the remaining oil to the skillet and place over medium heat. Add the onion and stir-fry for 4–5 minutes, then stir in the curry paste. Stir-fry for 1–2 minutes, then add the canned tomatoes and broth. Bring to a boil, reduce the heat to low, and let simmer gently, uncovered, for 10–15 minutes.

Add the koftas to the pan and stir carefully to coat them in the sauce. Simmer gently for 10–15 minutes, or until cooked through. Stir in the cream and cook for a final 2–3 minutes. Remove from the heat and garnish with the extra cilantro leaves. Serve with warm naan or steamed basmati rice.

3 tablespoons sunflower oil
1 onion, finely chopped
2 tablespoons medium curry paste
14 oz canned chopped tomatoes
¾ cup chicken broth
⅔ cup heavy cream

koftas

2 teaspoons finely grated fresh ginger
4 teaspoons crushed garlic
1 teaspoon ground cinnamon
½ cup freshly chopped cilantro leaves, plus extra to garnish
1¾ lb ground lamb, beef, or pork

serves 4

Kashmiri lamb kabobs

These succulent kabobs make for effortless entertaining, as they can be marinated up to 48 hours in advance and take a short time to cook. You can substitute the lamb with boneless beef, pork, or chicken. Serve with Onion, Cucumber & Tomato Relish and Cilantro & Mint Chutney (both page 88).

1¾ lb boneless lamb loin, cut into bite-size pieces
salt and freshly ground black pepper

marinade

2 shallots, finely chopped

2 teaspoons crushed garlic

2 teaspoons finely grated fresh ginger

1 tablespoon ground cumin

1 tablespoon ground coriander

1 tablespoon Kashmiri chili powder

1 tablespoon fennel seeds

6 tablespoons freshly chopped cilantro leaves

2 tablespoons freshly chopped mint leaves

1 cup heavy cream

½ teaspoon sugar

8–12 metal skewers
a baking sheet, lined with parchment paper

serves 4

Put the lamb in a large glass bowl. Put all the marinade ingredients in a food processor and blend until smooth. Season well. Pour over the lamb, cover, and marinate in the fridge for 24–48 hours.

When ready to cook, remove the bowl from the fridge and let come room temperature.

Preheat the oven to 400°F.

When ready to cook, thread the marinated lamb on to 8–12 metal skewers and arrange on the prepared baking sheet. Place in the preheated oven and cook for 12–15 minutes, or until tender and cooked through.

Serve with Onion, Cucumber & Tomato Relish and Cilantro & Mint Chutney.

lamb korma

This mild and creamy dish works equally well if you substitute the lamb for chicken. Serve with warm Naan (page 85) or steamed basmati rice.

4 tablespoons vegetable oil

1¾ lb boneless lamb loin, thinly sliced

1 onion, finely chopped

2 garlic cloves, finely chopped

2 teaspoons finely grated fresh ginger

½ cup ground almonds

1 tablespoon white poppy seeds (optional)

5 tablespoons Korma curry paste

⅔ cup lamb or chicken broth

1 cup light cream

2 tablespoons finely chopped pistachio nuts

1 tablespoon golden raisins

salt and freshly ground black pepper

crispy fried onions, to garnish

serves 4

Heat half the vegetable oil in a large, nonstick skillet and brown the lamb, in batches, for 2–3 minutes. Remove with a slotted spoon and set aside. Add the remaining oil to the skillet and cook the onion, garlic, and ginger over medium heat for 3–4 minutes.

Stir in the almonds, poppy seeds, if using, and curry paste and stir-fry for 1–2 minutes.

Add the lamb to the skillet with the broth and cream. Bring to a boil. Reduce the heat to low, season well, and simmer, uncovered, for about 30–40 minutes, stirring occasionally, until the lamb is tender.

Remove from the heat, stir in the pistachio nuts and raisins, and garnish with crispy fried onions. Serve with warm naan or steamed basmati rice.

ground beef & pea curry

Ground beef is cooked slowly with spices and peas resulting in a subtle, fragrant curry called "kheema mutter," which is great when accompanied by Tarka Dal (page 69), steamed basmati rice, or bread.

2 tablespoons sunflower oil

1 large onion, finely chopped

3 garlic cloves, crushed

1 teaspoon finely grated fresh ginger

3–4 green chiles (seeded if desired), thinly sliced

1 tablespoon cumin seeds

3 tablespoons medium curry paste

1¾ lb ground beef

14 oz canned chopped tomatoes

1 teaspoon sugar

¼ cup tomato paste

¼ cup coconut cream

8 oz frozen or fresh peas

salt and freshly ground black pepper

a large handful of cilantro leaves, chopped, to garnish

serves 4

Heat the sunflower oil in a large, heavy-based saucepan and add the onion. Cook over low heat for 15–20 minutes, until softened and just turning light golden. Add the garlic, ginger, chiles, cumin seeds, and curry paste and stir-fry over high heat for 1–2 minutes.

Add the ground beef and stir-fry for 3–4 minutes, then stir in the canned tomatoes, sugar, and tomato paste and bring to a boil. Season well, cover, and reduce the heat to low. Cook for 1–1½ hours. 10 minutes before the end of the cooking time, add the coconut cream and peas.

To serve, garnish with the cilantro and serve with Tarka Dal, steamed basmati rice, or bread.

beef madras

This fiery curry from southern India is not for the fainthearted although you can decrease the amounts of chile and curry powder to suit your palate. Serve with pickles as well as steamed basmati rice, if you like.

To make the marinade, combine the yogurt and curry powder in a glass bowl. Stir in the beef, season with salt, cover, and marinate in the fridge for 24 hours.

Heat the sunflower oil in a large, nonstick wok or skillet and add the bay leaf, cinnamon, cloves, and cardamom pods. Stir-fry for 1 minute, then add the onion. Stir-fry over medium heat for 4–5 minutes, then add the garlic, ginger, turmeric, red chile, chili powder, and cumin. Add the marinated beef (discarding the marinade) and stir-fry for 10–15 minutes over low heat.

Pour in the canned tomatoes and coconut milk and bring to a boil. Reduce the heat to low, cover tightly, and simmer gently for 1 hour, stirring occasionally. Stir in the garam masala 5 minutes before the end of cooking.

Check the seasoning. Drizzle with extra coconut milk and garnish with the cilantro. Serve with steamed basmati rice.

1¾ lb stewing beef, cut into large bite-size pieces
2 tablespoons sunflower oil
1 dried bay leaf
1 cinnamon stick
3 cloves
4 cardamom pods, bruised
1 large onion, thinly sliced
3 garlic cloves, crushed
1 teaspoon finely grated fresh ginger
1 teaspoon ground turmeric
1 red chile, split in half lengthwise
2 teaspoons hot chili powder
2 teaspoons ground cumin
7 oz canned chopped tomatoes
1¼ cups coconut milk, plus extra to drizzle
¼ teaspoon garam masala
salt and freshly ground black pepper
a small handful of cilantro leaves, chopped, to garnish

marinade
5 tablespoons plain yogurt
3 tablespoons Madras curry powder

serves 4

pork vindaloo

This fiery curry originates from the former Portuguese colony of Goa. The name is derived from the Portuguese for vinegar and garlic, the curry's main ingredients. Serve with steamed basmati rice.

To make the spice paste, put all the ingredients in a small food processor and blend to a paste. Transfer to a large glass bowl and add the pork. Rub the paste all over the pork pieces, cover, and marinate in the fridge for up to 24 hours.

To make the vindaloo, heat the sunflower oil in a large, heavy-based saucepan, then add the onion. Stir-fry for 3–4 minutes, then add the chili powder, turmeric, cumin, and marinated pork (discarding the spice paste). Stir-fry for 3–4 minutes, then stir in the potatoes, tomato paste, sugar, canned tomatoes, and broth. Season well and bring to a boil. Cover tightly and reduce the heat to low. Simmer gently for 1½ hours.

1¾ lb boneless pork shoulder, cut into bite-size pieces

salt and freshly ground black pepper

spice paste

2 teaspoons cumin seeds, toasted in a dry skillet

6 dried red chiles, broken into pieces

1 teaspoon cardamom seeds, crushed

1 cassia bark or cinnamon stick

10 black peppercorns

8 garlic cloves, finely grated

5 tablespoons white wine vinegar

vindaloo

2 tablespoons sunflower oil

1 onion, finely chopped

1 tablespoon medium or hot chili powder

1 teaspoon ground turmeric

2 teaspoons ground cumin

4 large potatoes, peeled and cut into chunks

⅓ cup tomato paste

1 tablespoon sugar

14 oz canned chopped tomatoes

¾ cup vegetable or chicken broth

serves 4

fish

Fish curries are particularly close to my heart. When I was a boy growing up in Mumbai, we had a cook responsible for making all the family meals, and Sunday was the only day my father was allowed (and time permitted him) to get in the kitchen and slave lovingly over a hot stove. So on that day we visited the food markets. Favorite among these was the fish market, from which we brought home just-caught fish and live crabs—these scraped and crawled on our kitchen table until it was time for them to jump into the cooking pot. As such, crab and fish curries such as **fish mollee (page 46)** have become cherished memories from my childhood. The sunny color and zingy flavor of **Goan shrimp curry (page 45)** are so incomparable that I seek it out before anything else whenever I go back to Goa. From delicate **tamarind & halibut curry (page 42)** to feisty **tandoori monkfish kabobs (page 38)** with its distinctively vibrant coloring, fish is infinitely versatile. And one of the greatest benefits of fish curries is their short cooking time: **lemon grass & scallop curry (page 43)** and the stunning **banana-leaf fish (page 41)** are guaranteed to become your favorite fast food. If you want all the punch of a curry but lighter, quicker, and fresher, fish is the ideal choice: just like a taste of sunshine even on the rainiest of evenings.

tandoori monkfish kabobs

Succulent pieces of monkfish are marinated in a blend of spices and yogurt, then quickly broiled. You could also grill these kabobs for an authentic smoky, tandoori flavor.

20 oz monkfish tail fillets, cut into bite-size pieces

4 red bell peppers, seeded and cut into bite-size pieces

freshly chopped cilantro, to garnish

freshly chopped mint, to garnish

lime wedges, to serve

thinly sliced red onions, to serve

tandoori marinade

1½ cups plain yogurt

2 tablespoons finely grated onion

1 tablespoon finely grated garlic

1 tablespoon finely grated fresh ginger

freshly squeezed juice of 2 limes

3 tablespoons tandoori spice powder or paste

¼ cup tomato paste

8 metal skewers

serves 4

To make the tandoori marinade, combine the yogurt, onion, garlic, ginger, lime juice, tandoori spice powder or paste, and tomato paste in a large glass bowl. Stir in the monkfish and bell peppers, cover, and refrigerate for 2–4 hours.

When ready to cook, thread the marinated monkfish and bell peppers on to the skewers and cook under a preheated medium broiler for 4–5 minutes on each side, or until the fish is just cooked through.

Garnish with the cilantro and mint and serve with lime wedges and sliced red onions on the side.

banana-leaf fish

Known as "patra ni macchi," these aromatic, banana-leaf wrapped fish packages are a famous Parsi preparation. If you cannot find banana leaves, use squares of oiled aluminum foil or parchment paper instead.

Preheat the oven to 400°F.

Cut the banana leaves into four 10-inch squares and soften them by dipping them in a pan of very hot water. Wipe the pieces dry when they are pliant.

To make the spice paste, grind the cumin, coriander, sugar, coconut, chiles, cilantro, mint, garlic, and ginger to a paste in a food processor or with a mortar and pestle.

Heat 1 tablespoon of the sunflower oil in a skillet and cook the paste over low heat until aromatic. Season with salt.

Lay the banana-leaf squares on a work surface. Spread the paste liberally over both sides of each piece of fish. Drizzle the lime juice over the top. Place a piece of fish on each banana leaf and wrap up like a package, securing it with skewers or twine. Place these packages on an oiled baking sheet and bake in the preheated oven for 15–20 minutes, or until the fish is just cooked through. Open out each fish package on its plate.

fresh banana leaves

3 tablespoons sunflower oil

4 thick halibut fillets (about 6½ oz each), skinned

freshly squeezed juice of 2 limes

salt

spice paste

2 teaspoons ground cumin

2 teaspoons ground coriander

1½ teaspoons Demerara sugar

5 oz freshly grated coconut

4 green chiles, seeded and chopped

8–10 tablespoons freshly chopped cilantro leaves

4 tablespoons freshly chopped mint leaves

5 garlic cloves, chopped

1 teaspoon finely grated fresh ginger

metal skewers or kitchen twine

serves 4

tamarind & halibut curry

This hearty curry can also be made with any thick, firm fish fillets, such as cod or salmon. Serve with steamed basmati rice and pappadoms, if you like.

To make the marinade, combine the tamarind paste, vinegar, cumin seeds, turmeric, chili powder, and salt in a shallow glass bowl. Stir in the fish, cover, and refrigerate for 25–30 minutes.

Meanwhile, heat a wok or large skillet over high heat and add the sunflower oil. Add the onion, garlic, ginger, and mustard seeds, reduce the heat to low, and cook for about 10 minutes, stirring occasionally.

Add the canned tomatoes and sugar and bring to a boil. Reduce the heat, cover, and cook gently for 15–20 minutes, stirring occasionally.

Add the fish and its marinade and stir gently to mix. Cover and simmer gently for 15–20 minutes, or until the fish is cooked through and flakes easily. Serve with steamed basmati rice and pappadoms.

1¾ lb thick halibut fillets, skinned and cubed

4 tablespoons sunflower oil

1 onion, finely chopped

3 garlic cloves, crushed

2 tablespoons finely grated fresh ginger

2 teaspoons black mustard seeds

two 14-oz cans chopped tomatoes

1 teaspoon sugar

marinade

1 tablespoon tamarind paste

¼ cup rice wine vinegar

2 tablespoons cumin seeds

1 teaspoon ground turmeric

1 teaspoon mild or medium chili powder

1 teaspoon salt

serves 4

lemon grass & scallop curry

Very fragrant and aromatic, this delicious curry is quick to whip up. Make sure you use only the freshest scallops.

Put the chili powder, coriander, cumin, garlic, shallots, lemon grass, galangal, palm sugar, shrimp paste, peanuts, and coconut milk in a blender and process until fairly smooth.

Put a large wok or skillet over high heat and add the spice mixture. Bring to a boil, reduce the heat to low, and simmer gently, uncovered, for 12–15 minutes, stirring occasionally.

Add the scallops and bring back to a boil. Reduce the heat to low and simmer gently for 6–8 minutes, or until the scallops are cooked through. Remove from the heat and scatter over some Thai basil leaves, chopped roasted peanuts, and chopped red chiles before serving.

1 tablespoon mild or medium chili powder

1 teaspoon ground coriander

2 teaspoons ground cumin

2 garlic cloves, crushed

6 small shallots, finely chopped

6 tablespoons finely chopped lemon grass

1 teaspoon finely grated galangal

1 tablespoon grated palm sugar

½ teaspoon shrimp paste

2 tablespoons finely chopped unroasted peanuts

2½ cups coconut milk

2¼ lb sea scallops

Thai sweet basil leaves, to garnish

chopped roasted peanuts, to garnish

chopped, seeded red chiles, to garnish

serves 4

2 tablespoons sunflower oil

2 onions, finely chopped

1 tablespoon finely grated fresh ginger

4 garlic cloves, crushed

2 red chiles (seeded if desired), thinly sliced

¼ teaspoon ground turmeric

2 teaspoons ground coriander

1 teaspoon medium or hot chili powder

2 teaspoons ground cumin

1 tablespoon tamarind paste

¾ cup coconut milk

1 teaspoon jaggery or brown sugar

2¼ lb raw jumbo shrimp, shelled and deveined but tails left intact

freshly chopped cilantro, to garnish

lime wedges, to serve

serves 4

Heat the sunflower oil in a large saucepan and add the onions. Cook over medium heat for 4–5 minutes, or until softened. Add the ginger, garlic, and chiles and stir-fry for 1–2 minutes.

Add the turmeric, coriander, chili powder, and cumin and stir-fry for 1–2 minutes.

Add the tamarind paste and coconut milk along with 1¼ cups water and bring to a boil. Add the jaggery, reduce the heat to low, and simmer gently for 15–20 minutes.

Add the shrimp to the pan and cook over high heat for 4–5 minutes, or until they turn pink and are cooked through. Season and remove from the heat. Garnish with the cilantro. Serve with lime wedges, steamed basmati rice, and pappadoms.

Goan shrimp curry

This simple and delicious shrimp curry evokes pictures of warm seas, sandy beaches, and swaying palm trees. Serve with steamed basmati rice and pappadoms and wash it all down with an ice-cold beer for maximum indulgence.

fish mollee

Kerala on the west coast of India is home to this creamy, mild, and very flavorsome fish curry. Use any firm, thick white fish or shrimp as you like. Serve with steamed basmati rice.

Put the onion, garlic, chiles, cumin, coriander, turmeric, cilantro, and ¾ cup water in a food processor and blend until smooth.

Heat the sunflower oil in a large, heavy-based skillet, add the curry leaves, and stir-fry for 20–30 seconds. Add the blended mixture, stir, and cook over high heat for 3–4 minutes. Turn the heat to low, add the coconut milk, and simmer gently, uncovered, for 20 minutes.

Add the fish to the skillet in a single layer and bring the mixture back to a boil. Reduce the heat to low and simmer gently for 5–6 minutes, or until the fish is just cooked through. Season and remove from the heat. Garnish with deep-fried curry leaves and serve with steamed basmati rice.

1 onion, coarsely chopped

4 garlic cloves, crushed

2 green chiles, seeded and finely chopped

1 tablespoon ground cumin

1 teaspoon ground coriander

1 teaspoon ground turmeric

a big handful of cilantro leaves, finely chopped

2 tablespoons sunflower oil

6 fresh curry leaves

1½ cups coconut milk

4 thick halibut or cod fillets (about 6½ oz each), skinned

salt and freshly ground black pepper

deep-fried curry leaves, to garnish

serves 4

vegetables

From Kerala in the southern tip of India, via Mumbai on the western coast, to Punjab in the north and a leap eastwards to Thailand, Asia has a treasure trove of vegetable curries on offer: try deep, heady, tomatoey **spiced eggplants (page 51)** or the delicate fragrance of **vegetable stew (page 56)**—both guarantee an explosion of flavors in your mouth. And take inspiration from street vendors all over India who sell snacks such as **onion bhajis (page 61)** and **spicy potato balls (page 60)** stuffed in a roll with chutney. Side dish **(saag paneer, page 62)** or vegetarian option **(okra masala, page 55)**, there is a vegetable recipe to suit every mood and occasion. If you want to do as Indians do, you must include a vegetable dish, such as **cauliflower masala (page 52)** with your curry. In India, a typical meal consists of rice, bread, vegetables, dal, and a meat or fish curry, all served at the same time, and all there to provide a spectrum of taste sensations. So next time you are planning a feast for friends, why not surprise everyone with a flaming **Thai red pumpkin curry (page 59)** or a simple **tomato & egg curry (page 53)** and a host of accompaniments—swap roast potatoes for **spiced potatoes (page 62)** and boring boiled cabbage for beautifully spiced **Punjabi cabbage (page 65)**. You'll find every plate scraped clean at the end of the meal!

spiced eggplants

Eggplants are cooked in pickling spices in this warming dish. Serve it with yogurt and steamed basmati rice and it becomes an ideal vegetarian entrée.

Put the ginger, garlic, and half the canned tomatoes in a blender and blend until smooth. Set aside.

Heat half the sunflower oil in a large, heavy-based skillet, then add as many eggplants as you can fit in a single layer, cut-side down. Cook over medium heat for 3–4 minutes, or until lightly browned, then turn over and cook for a further 3–4 minutes. Remove with a slotted spoon and drain on paper towels. Repeat with the remaining oil and cook the remaining eggplants. Remove from the skillet and drain on paper towels.

Reheat the oil that is left in the skillet and add the fennel seeds and nigella seeds. Stir-fry for 1–2 minutes, then add the blended tomato mixture. Stir-fry for 2–3 minutes, then add the remaining canned tomatoes, the coriander, turmeric, and paprika. Season well. Cook over medium heat, stirring often, for 6–8 minutes, until the mixture is smooth and thick.

Add the reserved eggplants to the skillet and toss gently until evenly coated. Cover and cook gently for 10–12 minutes. Remove from the heat and let rest for 10–15 minutes before serving. Garnish with the cilantro and serve with steamed basmati rice and a little yogurt on the side.

1 tablespoon finely grated fresh ginger

2 tablespoons crushed garlic

14 oz canned chopped tomatoes

1 cup sunflower oil

1½ lb baby eggplants, halved lengthwise

2 teaspoons fennel seeds

2 teaspoons nigella seeds

1 tablespoon ground coriander

¼ teaspoon ground turmeric

1 teaspoon paprika

salt and freshly ground black pepper

freshly chopped cilantro leaves, to garnish

serves 4

cauliflower masala

In this simple dish, cauliflower florets are stir-fried in a seasoned, spiced oil until just tender. Substitute broccoli florets if desired, to ring the changes.

1 tablespoon sunflower oil
2 teaspoons cumin seeds
1 teaspoon black mustard seeds
1 lb cauliflower florets
2 garlic cloves, thinly sliced
2 teaspoons finely chopped
fresh ginger
1 green chile, thinly sliced
1 teaspoon garam masala
⅔ cup hot water
freshly squeezed juice of ½ lemon
salt and freshly ground black pepper

serves 4

Heat the sunflower oil in a large skillet over medium heat. Add the cumin seeds and mustard seeds. Stir-fry for 30 seconds, then add the cauliflower, garlic, ginger, and chile. Turn the heat to high and stir-fry for 6–8 minutes, or until the cauliflower is lightly browned at the edges.

Stir in the garam masala and hot water and stir well. Cover and cook over high heat for 1–2 minutes.

Season well and drizzle with the lemon juice just before serving.

tomato & egg curry

This tasty curry from Mumbai is quick to prepare and makes good use of everyday kitchen staples. Serve with steamed basmati rice.

4 potatoes, peeled and cut into bite-size pieces

2 tablespoons sunflower oil

1 tablespoon black mustard seeds

2 garlic cloves, crushed

2 dried red chiles

10 fresh curry leaves

1 onion, thinly sliced

2 tablespoons medium curry powder

1 tablespoon ground coriander

1 tablespoon cumin seeds

½ teaspoon ground turmeric

14 oz canned chopped tomatoes

1 teaspoon sugar

¾ cup coconut milk

8 eggs, hard-boiled and peeled

salt

serves 4

Cook the potatoes in a pan of salted boiling water until tender.

Heat the sunflower oil in a large, nonstick wok or skillet. Add the mustard seeds and when they start to pop, add the garlic, chiles, and curry leaves and sauté for 1 minute. Add the onion and cook, stirring constantly, for 5–6 minutes.

Stir in the curry powder, coriander, cumin seeds, and turmeric, then stir in the canned tomatoes and sugar. Bring to a boil, reduce the heat to medium, and cook for 8–10 minutes, stirring often.

Add the coconut milk, eggs, and potatoes. Cook gently for 8–10 minutes, until the sauce has thickened. Season with salt and serve with steamed basmati rice.

okra masala

When shopping for the okra, make sure that they are bright green, firm, and not bruised. This dish makes a fantastic vegetarian entrée when accompanied by steamed basmati rice, dal, and pickles.

Heat the sunflower oil in a large, nonstick wok or skillet over medium heat and add the curry leaves, mustard seeds, and onion. Stir-fry for 3–4 minutes, then add the cumin, coriander, curry powder, and turmeric. Stir-fry for 1–2 minutes, then add the garlic and okra. Stir and cook over high heat for 2–3 minutes.

Stir in the tomatoes and season well. Cover, reduce the heat to low, and cook gently for 10–12 minutes, stirring occasionally, until the okra is tender.

Garnish with the grated coconut before serving with steamed basmati rice, dal, and pickles.

2 tablespoons sunflower oil

6–8 fresh curry leaves

2 teaspoons black mustard seeds

1 onion, finely diced

2 teaspoons ground cumin

1 teaspoon ground coriander

2 teaspoons medium curry powder

1 teaspoon ground turmeric

3 garlic cloves, finely chopped

1 lb okra, trimmed and cut diagonally into 1-inch pieces

2 ripe plum tomatoes, finely chopped

3 tablespoons freshly grated coconut

serves 4

vegetable stew

This fragrant and mild vegetable and coconut stew is called "avial" in its home town of Kerala, in the southern tip of India. Traditionally served with steamed rice pancakes, it is equally good eaten with rice or bread.

2 tablespoons sunflower oil
6 shallots, thinly sliced
2 teaspoons black mustard seeds
8–10 fresh curry leaves
1 green chile, thinly sliced
2 teaspoons finely grated fresh ginger
1 teaspoon ground turmeric
2 teaspoons ground cumin
6 black peppercorns
2 carrots, cut into thick matchsticks
1 zucchini, cut into thick matchsticks
6½ oz green beans
1 large potato, peeled and cut into thick matchsticks
1¼ cups coconut milk
½ cup vegetable broth or water
freshly squeezed juice of ½ lemon
salt and freshly ground black pepper

serves 4

Heat the sunflower oil in a large, heavy-based skillet and add the shallots. Stir and cook over medium heat for 4–5 minutes. Add the mustard seeds, curry leaves, chile, ginger, turmeric, cumin, and peppercorns and stir-fry for 1–2 minutes.

Add the carrots, zucchini, beans, and potato to the skillet along with the coconut milk and broth and bring to a boil. Reduce the heat, cover, and cook gently for 12–15 minutes, or until the vegetables are tender.

Season well and drizzle with the lemon juice just before serving with steamed basmati rice or bread.

Thai red pumpkin curry

You can use butternut squash in this curry instead of the pumpkin if you prefer. To elaborate on the dish for a dinner party, thrown in some cooked jumbo shrimp 5 minutes before the end of the cooking time.

Heat the sunflower oil in a large, nonstick wok or skillet. Add the onion, garlic, and ginger and stir-fry for 3–4 minutes. Stir in the curry paste and pumpkin and stir-fry for 3–4 minutes.

Pour in the coconut milk, broth, lime leaves, palm sugar, and lemon grass. Bring to a boil, then reduce the heat to low and simmer gently for 20–25 minutes, stirring occasionally, or until the pumpkin is tender.

Season well and garnish with the Thai basil leaves and shredded lime leaves just before serving.

2 tablespoons sunflower oil

1 red onion, thinly sliced

2 garlic cloves, crushed

1 teaspoon finely grated fresh ginger

3 tablespoons Thai red curry paste

1¾ lb pumpkin flesh, cut into bite-size pieces

1⅔ cups coconut milk

⅔ cup vegetable broth

6 kaffir lime leaves, plus extra, shredded, to garnish

2 teaspoons grated palm sugar

3 lemon grass stalks, bruised

salt and freshly ground black pepper

Thai sweet basil leaves, to garnish

serves 4

spicy potato balls

This savory potato snack, called "batata vadas," is a popular street food all over India. Serve them with a bowl of the Cilantro & Mint Chutney (page 88) for dipping.

Cook the potatoes in a pan of salted boiling water until tender.

Heat the sunflower oil in a large skillet over medium heat, then add the cumin seeds and mustard seeds and stir-fry for 1–2 minutes. Add the onion, ginger, and chiles and stir-fry for 3–4 minutes. Add the potatoes and peas and stir-fry for 3–4 minutes. Season and stir in the lemon juice and cilantro. Divide the mixture into 20 portions and shape each one into a ball. Chill until ready to use.

Combine the gram flour and self-rising flour in a bowl. Season and stir in the turmeric and coriander seeds. Gradually whisk in 1½ cups water to make a fairly smooth and thick batter.

Fill a heavy-based saucepan one-third full with sunflower oil and heat to 350°F or until a piece of bread dropped in sizzles and browns within 10 seconds. Dip the potato balls in the batter, then carefully lower them into the hot oil in batches. Deep-fry for 1–2 minutes, or until golden. Drain on paper towels and serve warm with Cilantro & Mint Chutney.

1¼ lb potatoes, peeled and diced

1 tablespoon sunflower oil, plus extra for deep-frying

4 teaspoons cumin seeds

1 teaspoon black mustard seeds

1 small onion, finely chopped

2 teaspoons finely grated fresh ginger

2 green chiles, seeded and chopped

1¼ cups shelled fresh peas

freshly squeezed juice of 1 lemon

6 tablespoons freshly chopped cilantro leaves

⅔ cup gram flour (besan, or ground chickpeas)

6 tablespoons self-rising flour

a large pinch of ground turmeric

2 teaspoons coriander seeds, crushed

salt and freshly ground black pepper

makes 20

onion bhajis

A popular accompaniment to a takeaway curry, onion bhajis are irresistible. When they are freshly made and served with Cucumber & Yogurt Relish (page 88), they make the perfect vegetarian snack food.

Combine the gram flour, chili powder, turmeric, coriander seeds, and a pinch of salt in a bowl. Gradually add enough water to make a thick batter that will hold the onion together. Mix the onions and curry leaves into the batter.

Fill a heavy-based saucepan one-third full with sunflower oil and heat to 350°F or until a piece of bread dropped in sizzles and browns within 10 seconds. Take spoonfuls of the onion batter and carefully lower them into the hot oil in batches. Deep-fry for 1–2 minutes, or until golden all over and cooked through. Drain on paper towels. Sprinkle with salt and serve warm with Cucumber & Yogurt Relish.

2 cups gram flour (besan, or ground chickpeas)
1 teaspoon chili powder (mild, medium, or hot, as desired)
1 teaspoon ground turmeric
1 tablespoon coriander seeds, crushed
3 large onions, sliced
6 fresh curry leaves
sunflower oil, for deep-frying
salt

makes about 15

spiced potatoes

This spiced potato dish from Mumbai is terrific when served with Poori (page 84) and Cilantro & Mint Chutney (page 88) for a light snack or a Sunday brunch with a difference.

1 lb potatoes, peeled and cubed
¼ cup sunflower oil
2 teaspoons black mustard seeds
1 teaspoon medium or hot chili powder, or paprika
4 teaspoons cumin seeds
8–10 fresh curry leaves
2 teaspoons ground cumin
2 teaspoons ground coriander
1 teaspoon ground turmeric
6 tablespoons freshly chopped cilantro leaves
freshly squeezed lemon juice, to taste
salt and freshly ground black pepper

serves 4

Cook the potatoes in a pan of salted boiling water until tender.

Heat the sunflower oil in a large, nonstick wok or skillet. Add the mustard seeds, chili powder, cumin seeds, and curry leaves. Stir-fry for 1–2 minutes, then add the ground cumin, coriander, turmeric, and potatoes. Season well and stir-fry over high heat for 4–5 minutes.

Stir in the cilantro and lemon juice, to taste, and serve with poori and Cilantro & Mint Chutney.

saag paneer

Paneer is an Indian cow's milk cheese easily found in Asian stores. Here it is paired with spinach and tomato for a popular Indian dish.

1 lb frozen spinach
3 tablespoons ghee or butter
2 teaspoons cumin seeds
1 onion, very finely chopped
2 plum tomatoes, finely chopped
2 teaspoons crushed garlic
1 tablespoon finely grated fresh ginger
1 teaspoon chili powder (mild, medium, or hot, as desired)
1 teaspoon ground coriander
8 oz paneer, cut into bite-size pieces
2 tablespoons heavy cream
2 tablespoons freshly chopped cilantro leaves
1 teaspoon freshly squeezed lemon juice
salt and freshly ground black pepper

serves 4

Bring a large saucepan of water to a boil. Add the frozen spinach and bring back to a boil. Cook for 2–3 minutes, then drain thoroughly. Transfer to a food processor and blend until smooth.

Heat the ghee in a large, heavy-based skillet. Add the cumin seeds and onion and stir-fry for 6–8 minutes over medium/low heat until the onion turns lightly golden. Add the tomatoes, garlic, ginger, chili powder, and coriander. Season well. Stir-fry for 2–3 minutes. Add the paneer and cook for 30–40 seconds over high heat. Add the blended spinach and stir-fry for 4–5 minutes. Stir in the cream, cilantro, and lemon juice.

Punjabi cabbage

Eaten widely in Punjab and northern India, green cabbage is quick to cook and excellent served with any main vegetarian or meat dishes.

Heat the sunflower oil in a large, nonstick wok or skillet over low heat. Add the shallots, ginger, garlic, and chiles and stir-fry for 2–3 minutes, or until the shallots have softened.

Add the cumin seeds, turmeric, and coriander seeds and stir-fry for 1 minute.

Turn the heat to high and add the cabbage, tossing well to coat in the spice mixture. Add the curry powder and season well. Cover and cook over medium heat for 10 minutes, stirring occasionally. Stir in the ghee and serve.

3 tablespoons sunflower oil

4 shallots, finely chopped

2 teaspoons finely grated fresh ginger

2 teaspoons crushed garlic

2 green chiles, halved lengthwise

2 teaspoons cumin seeds

1 teaspoon ground turmeric

1 teaspoon coriander seeds, crushed

1 lb green or white cabbage, shredded

1 tablespoon mild or medium curry powder

1 tablespoon ghee or butter

salt and freshly ground black pepper

serves 4

beans

Imagine a glorious helping of comfort food—not macaroni cheese, Mom's mashed potatoes, or your signature dish of toast, but **chickpea masala (page 70)**, slow-cooked to perfection, or a bowl of red split lentils and rice spiked with warming spices—**kitcheree (page 72)** which evolved into kedgeree as we know it today. There's something about beans, peas, and lentils (dal in Indian) which render a dish hearty, wholesome, and somehow meaty without the need for any meat. So integral are they to the Indian diet that they deserve a chapter all of their own. By themselves, lentils, chickpeas, and kidney beans lack punch, but team them up with the likes of turmeric, cumin, chiles, curry leaves, and ginger, and you get a magical **tarka dal (page 69)**. One of my abiding memories from childhood is of our cook crushing and pounding wet and dry spices on a granite grinding stone with a kind of rolling pin. The colors and fragrances produced in this arduous process were unforgettable, and made it a real labor of love. **Spiced eggplant dal (page 73)** benefits from being made a day in advance, and in fact many lentils and beans do need soaking overnight, such as in the **spinach dal (page 69)**, but you can cheat the **red kidney bean curry (page 74)** by using good-quality organic canned beans instead.

tarka dal

This is the ultimate Indian comfort food. Cooked lentils are given a final seasoning with a spiced oil called "tarka" to give the dish its distinctive flavor.

1¼ cups dried red split lentils
1 teaspoon ground turmeric
4 ripe tomatoes, roughly chopped
6–8 tablespoons freshly chopped cilantro leaves

tarka

¼ cup sunflower oil
2 teaspoons black mustard seeds
3 teaspoons cumin seeds
2 garlic cloves, very thinly sliced
2 teaspoons very finely chopped fresh ginger
6–8 fresh curry leaves
1 dried red chile
2 teaspoons ground cumin
2 teaspoons ground coriander
salt and freshly ground black pepper

serves 4

Rinse the lentils until the water runs clear. Place in a heavy-based saucepan with 4 cups water. Bring to a boil over high heat, skimming off any scum that rises to the surface. Lower the heat and cook for 20–25 minutes. Remove from the heat and using a handheld blender or whisk, blend until smooth. Return to the heat and stir in the turmeric and tomatoes. Bring to a boil, season, and stir in the cilantro. To make the tarka, heat the sunflower oil in a skillet. Add all the ingredients and stir-fry for 1–2 minutes. Stir into the dal.

spinach dal

Also known as "kali dal" (which means whole black lentils) this simple yet scrumptious dish is a staple food across India. Serve with bread and pickles.

⅔ cup dried black lentils
3 tablespoons butter
1 onion, finely chopped
3 garlic cloves, crushed
2 teaspoons finely grated fresh ginger
2 green chiles, halved lengthwise
1 teaspoon ground turmeric
1 teaspoon paprika
1 tablespoon ground coriander
1 tablespoon ground cumin
6½ oz canned red kidney beans, drained and rinsed
6½ oz baby leaf spinach
a large handful of cilantro leaves, chopped
⅔ cup heavy cream

serves 4

Rinse the lentils. Drain, place in a deep bowl, and cover with cold water. Let soak for 10–12 hours. Rinse the lentils, then place in a saucepan with 2 cups boiling water. Bring to a boil, reduce the heat, and simmer for 35–40 minutes, or until tender. Drain and set aside. Melt the butter in a saucepan and stir-fry the onion, garlic, ginger, and chiles for 5–6 minutes, then add the turmeric, paprika, coriander, cumin, kidney beans, and lentils. Add 2 cups water and bring to a boil. Reduce the heat and stir in the spinach. Cook gently for 10–15 minutes, stirring often. Stir in the cilantro and cream.

chickpea masala

This street food of spiced chickpeas is served at little food stalls in the bazaars and markets all over India. Usually eaten with Poori (page 84), it makes a great accompaniment to any Indian meal.

Heat the sunflower oil in a large, heavy-based skillet over medium heat and add the garlic, ginger, onion, and chiles. Stir-fry for 6–8 minutes, or until the onion is lightly golden. Add the chili powder, cumin, coriander, yogurt, and garam masala and stir-fry for 1–2 minutes.

Stir in 2 cups water and bring to a boil. Add the tamarind paste, curry powder, and chickpeas and bring back to a boil. Reduce the heat to low and simmer gently for 30–40 minutes, stirring occasionally, or until the liquid has reduced, coating the chickpeas in a dark, rich sauce.

Serve in little bowls drizzled with a little whisked yogurt, garnished with cilantro and chili powder, and with lemon wedges on the side.

¼ cup sunflower oil

4 garlic cloves, crushed

2 teaspoons finely grated fresh ginger

1 large onion, coarsely grated

1–2 green chiles, thinly sliced

1 teaspoon hot chili powder, plus extra to garnish

1 tablespoon ground cumin

1 tablespoon ground coriander

3 tablespoons plain yogurt, plus extra, whisked, to drizzle

2 teaspoons garam masala

2 teaspoons tamarind paste

2 teaspoons medium curry powder

two 14-oz cans chickpeas, drained and rinsed

freshly chopped cilantro leaves, to garnish

lemon wedges, to serve

serves 4

kitcheree

This dish began life as a simple combination of lentils cooked with rice and a few spices. In the British Raj, it was taken to a different level with the addition of smoked fish and boiled eggs and called kedgeree. Serve with pickles, if you like.

Rinse the lentils and rice until the water runs clear. Drain thoroughly.

Heat the sunflower oil in a heavy-based saucepan and add the onion. Stir-fry for 6–8 minutes over medium heat, then add the turmeric, cumin seeds, chile, cinnamon, cloves, and cardamom pods. Continue to stir-fry for 2–3 minutes, then add the rice and lentils. Stir-fry for 2–3 minutes, then add the stock and cilantro. Season well and bring to a boil. Reduce the heat to low, cover tightly, and cook for 10 minutes. Remove from the heat and let stand undisturbed for another 10 minutes.

Transfer to a serving dish and serve with yogurt and pickles on the side.

½ cup dried red split lentils
1¼ cups basmati rice
3 tablespoons sunflower oil
1 onion, finely chopped
1 teaspoon ground turmeric
1 tablespoon cumin seeds
1 dried red chile
1 cinnamon stick
3 cloves
3 cardamom pods, lightly bruised
2 cups vegetable broth
½ cup freshly chopped cilantro leaves
salt and freshly ground black pepper
natural yogurt, to serve

serves 4

spiced eggplant dal

Dals can be made from many different varieties of lentils. Here we use the yellow split lentils which require no soaking and cook quickly. It benefits from being made a day in advance, which gives the flavors time to mingle and mellow. Serve with steamed basmati rice or bread.

Heat the sunflower oil in a saucepan over high heat. Add the onions and stir-fry for 6–8 minutes, until they start to become golden. Reduce the heat and stir in the garlic, ginger, cumin seeds, mustard seeds, and curry powder. Stir-fry for 1–2 minutes, then add the lentils and 2½ cups water. Bring to a boil, add the eggplant and cherry tomatoes, and reduce the heat to low. Cover and simmer gently for 25–30 minutes, stirring occasionally, until the dal is thick and the lentils are tender.

Season well with salt and stir in the cilantro. Serve with steamed basmati rice or bread.

3 tablespoons sunflower oil
2 onions, finely chopped
4 garlic cloves, finely chopped
1 teaspoon finely grated fresh ginger
1 tablespoon cumin seeds
1 tablespoon black mustard seeds
2 tablespoons curry powder
(mild, medium, or hot, as desired)
a scant cup dried yellow split lentils
1 eggplant, cut into bite-size pieces
8 cherry tomatoes
½ cup freshly chopped cilantro leaves
salt

serves 4

red kidney bean curry

Dried red kidney beans are turned into the perfect comfort food, in this lightly spiced curry. If pressed for time, you can use very good-quality organic canned red kidney beans instead.

Put the red kidney beans in a large saucepan, cover with cold water, and let soak overnight.

Drain the soaked beans and return to the saucepan with double the amount of water. Bring to a boil, then keep boiling for 15 minutes. Reduce the heat to medium/low and simmer gently for 1 hour, or until the beans are tender. Drain, reserving the cooking liquid.

Heat the butter and sunflower oil in a large, heavy-based saucepan and add the onion, cinnamon, bay leaves, garlic, and ginger and stir-fry for 4–5 minutes. Stir in the turmeric, coriander, cumin, garam masala, and chiles.

Add the beans, tomato paste, and enough of the reserved cooking liquid to make a thick sauce. Bring to a boil and cook for 4–5 minutes, stirring often.

Season well, drizzle with whisked yogurt, if desired, and garnish with cilantro.

1¼ cups dried red kidney beans
1 tablespoon butter
2 tablespoons sunflower oil
1 onion, finely chopped
a 2-inch piece of cinnamon stick or cassia bark
2 dried bay leaves
3 garlic cloves, crushed
2 teaspoons finely grated fresh ginger
½ teaspoon ground turmeric
1 teaspoon ground coriander
2 teaspoons ground cumin
1 teaspoon garam masala
2 dried red chiles
¼ cup tomato paste
salt and freshly ground black pepper
whisked yogurt, to drizzle (optional)
freshly chopped cilantro leaves, to serve

serves 4

rice & breads

One of the most irresistible things about curry is the sauce which often accompanies it, so it follows that you will need something on the side for scooping or soaking up. Punchy or barely there, light as air or densely satisfying—rice and breads have everything to offer. In fact, even the simplest curry simply wouldn't be right without **lemon** or **coconut rice (both page 78)** or fluffy **naan (page 85)** on the side. So tasty are the flatbreads, for example, that it is common in India to snack on a freshly cooked **saag roti (page 84)** with a generous dollop of chutney. I can't recommend it enough. Delicate, puffed-up **poori (page 84)** complement spicy potatoes and fish curries beautifully. And **morel mushroom pulao (page 82)** is a rice dish with a difference—smoky morsels of morels amidst cinnamon- and cardamom-scented basmati. Meanwhile, **lamb biryani (page 81)** is usually reserved as a special-occasion dish since it takes a while to cook. During festivals such as Diwali, huge pots of biryani are placed over coals along the street and their lids are carefully sealed in place with a flour-and-water mixture to ensure that no flavors or heat are lost during cooking, resulting in the tenderest chunks of lamb and fluffiest rice. An entire one-pot meal, lovingly prepared and left to steam to a meltingly soft consistency.

lemon rice

A typical southern Indian favorite, this citrussy rice dish is a perfect accompaniment to plain broiled fish or chicken, or steamed vegetables.

1¼ cups basmati rice
1 tablespoon light olive oil
12–14 fresh curry leaves
1 dried red chile
2 cassia barks or cinnamon sticks
2–3 cloves
4–6 cardamom pods, bruised
2 teaspoons cumin seeds
¼ teaspoon ground turmeric
freshly squeezed juice of 1 large lemon
2 cups boiling water
salt and freshly ground black pepper

serves 4

Rinse the rice until the water runs clear. Drain thoroughly and set aside.

Heat the olive oil in a nonstick saucepan and add the curry leaves, chile, cassia, cloves, cardamom pods, cumin seeds, and turmeric. Stir-fry for 20–30 seconds, then add the rice. Stir-fry for 2 minutes, then add the lemon juice and boiling water. Season well and bring to a boil. Cover the pan tightly, reduce the heat to low, and cook for 10–12 minutes.

Let stand undisturbed for 10 minutes. Fluff up the rice with a fork and season.

coconut rice

This aromatic and mildly flavored rice dish acts as a perfect foil to any spicy curry.

1¼ cups basmati rice
2 tablespoons sunflower oil
2 teaspoons black mustard seeds
2 teaspoons cumin seeds
2 dried red chiles
10 fresh curry leaves
2¼ cups hot water
¼ cup coconut cream
2 tablespoons freshly grated coconut, to garnish

serves 4

Rinse the rice until the water runs clear. Transfer to a bowl, cover with cold water, and let soak for 15 minutes. Drain thoroughly.

Heat the sunflower oil in a heavy-based saucepan and add the mustard seeds, cumin seeds, chiles, and curry leaves. Stir-fry for 30 seconds, then add the hot water and coconut cream. Stir well and bring to a boil. Reduce the heat to low, cover tightly, and cook for 10 minutes.

Let stand undisturbed for 10 minutes. Fluff up the rice with a fork and scatter over the grated coconut.

lamb biryani

This one-pot rice and lamb preparation was traditionally cooked during royal festival days. It can be made with chicken, seafood, or vegetables too. Serve with Onion, Cucumber & Tomato Relish or Cucumber & Yogurt Relish (both page 88) for maximum enjoyment!

To make the marinade, combine the garlic, ginger, yogurt, and cilantro in a glass bowl. Add the lamb and rub the marinade into the lamb pieces. Cover and marinate in the fridge for 4–6 hours.

Heat the sunflower oil in a heavy-based pan, add the onion, and cook for 12–15 minutes, until lightly golden. Add the marinated lamb and cook over high heat for 15 minutes, stirring often. Stir in the coriander, cumin, chili powder, turmeric, and canned tomatoes, season well, and bring to a boil. Reduce the heat to low and simmer gently for 30 minutes, or until the lamb is tender and most of the liquid has been absorbed. Set aside.

Prepare the rice. Heat the sunflower oil in a heavy-based pan. Add the cumin seeds, onion, cloves, peppercorns, cardamom pods, and cinnamon and stir-fry for 6–8 minutes. Add the rice and stir-fry for 2 minutes. Pour in 1⅔ cups water and bring to a boil. Cover and simmer gently for 6–7 minutes. Set aside. Mix the saffron and milk and set aside.

Preheat the oven to 350°F.

Put a thin layer of the meat mixture in the casserole dish and cover with half the rice. Drizzle over half the saffron mixture. Top with the remaining lamb mixture and cover with the remaining rice. Drizzle over the remaining saffron mixture, cover the dish with foil, then cover with the lid. Bake in the preheated oven for 30 minutes. Remove from the oven and let rest, still covered, for 30 minutes before serving.

1 lb boneless lamb, from the leg, cut into bite-size pieces

¼ cup sunflower oil

1 onion, finely chopped

1 tablespoon ground coriander

1 teaspoon ground cumin

1 teaspoon mild or medium chili powder

1 teaspoon ground turmeric

6 oz canned chopped tomatoes

marinade

4 garlic cloves, crushed

1 teaspoon finely grated fresh ginger

⅔ cup plain yogurt

6 tablespoons freshly chopped cilantro leaves

rice

¼ cup sunflower oil

2 teaspoons cumin seeds

1 onion, thinly sliced

6 cloves

10 black peppercorns

4 cardamom pods

1 cinnamon stick

1¼ cups basmati rice

1 teaspoon saffron threads

3 tablespoons warm milk

an ovenproof casserole dish with a tight-fitting lid, lightly buttered

serves 4

morel mushroom pulao

"Gucchi" is the name for the wild morel mushrooms found in the forests of Kashmir. They are extremely expensive to buy fresh, so smoky dried morels are used in this rich rice dish.

Put the mushrooms in a glass bowl with the boiling water. Cover and let stand for 20–30 minutes, or until the mushrooms have re-hydrated and are soft. Strain the mushrooms through a fine strainer, reserving the liquid.

Rinse the rice until the water runs clear. Transfer to a bowl, cover with cold water, and let soak for 20 minutes. Drain thoroughly.

Heat the sunflower oil in a heavy-based saucepan and add the cinnamon, cumin seeds, cloves, cardamom pods, peppercorns, and dried onions. Stir-fry for 2–3 minutes, then add the drained mushrooms and the peas. Stir-fry for 2–3 minutes, then add the rice. Pour in the reserved mushroom liquid and season well. Bring to a boil, cover tightly, and reduce the heat to low. Cook for 8–10 minutes, then remove from the heat and let stand, covered, for 10 minutes. Fluff up the rice with a fork before serving.

1 oz dried morel mushrooms
2½ cups boiling water
1⅓ cups basmati rice
¼ cup sunflower oil
1 cinnamon stick
2 teaspoons cumin seeds
2 cloves
4 cardamom pods, lightly bruised
8 black peppercorns
¼ cup dried onions
1¼ cups frozen peas
salt and freshly ground black pepper

serves 4

poori

These deep-fried whole-grain breads are usually eaten with spicy potatoes or seafood curries. They are sometimes also eaten with a sweet yogurt dessert called "shrikand."

2 cups whole-wheat flour
a pinch of salt
2 tablespoons ghee, melted
sunflower oil, for deep-frying

makes 20

Combine the flour and salt in a large bowl. Add the ghee and a little cold water (¼–⅓ cup) to make a stiff dough. Cover with a damp cloth and refrigerate for 30 minutes.

Divide the dough into 20 portions and shape each one into a ball. Flatten them with the palm of your hand, then roll out into a 4-inch disk.

Fill a large wok one-third full with sunflower oil and heat over moderate heat to 350°F or until a piece of bread dropped in sizzles and browns within 10 seconds. Carefully drop in the pooris in batches and deep-fry for 1–2 minutes on each side, or until puffed up and golden. Remove with a slotted spoon and drain on paper towels. Eat immediately.

saag roti

These flatbreads are made with chapatti flour (atta), available from Asian stores. If you can't find it, use an equal mix of whole-wheat and all-purpose flour.

3½ oz zucchini, coarsely grated
3½ oz baby spinach leaves, roughly chopped
3¾ cups chapatti flour (atta), plus extra to dust
a large pinch of salt
1 tablespoon cumin seeds, lightly toasted in a dry skillet
1 red chile, seeded and finely chopped
4 tablespoons ghee or melted butter
sunflower oil, for brushing

makes 20

Put the grated zucchini in a strainer and squeeze out as much liquid as you can. Put the flesh in a mixing bowl. Blanch the spinach in a large saucepan of boiling water until just wilted, drain thoroughly, and squeeze out as much liquid as you can. Add the spinach to the zucchini.

Sift the flour into a bowl with the salt. Stir in the cumin seeds, chile, and zucchini and spinach mixture. Stir in the ghee along with 1 cup lukewarm water. Mix to form a soft, pliable dough, then turn out onto a floured surface and knead for 4–5 minutes. Transfer to an oiled bowl, cover, and let rest for 30 minutes.

Divide the dough into 20 pieces. Roll out each piece to a 5-inch disk about ¼ inch thick. Heat a large, heavy-based skillet until hot, lightly brush with oil, and cook one at a time for 1–2 minutes on each side, until lightly blistered and cooked through. Cover with a kitchen towel and keep warm while you cook the rest. Serve with Tarka Dal and any curry.

naan

Naan is one of the most popular leavened breads from India, traditionally cooked in a tandoori or clay oven. It works just as well under a broiler.

3½ cups self-rising flour
2 teaspoons sugar
1 teaspoon salt
1 teaspoon baking powder
8 tablespoons melted butter or ghee, plus extra for brushing
1 cup milk, warmed
2 tablespoons nigella seeds

makes 8

Sift the flour, sugar, salt, and baking powder into a large bowl. Add the melted butter and rub into the flour mixture with your fingers. Gradually add the warm milk and mix until you get a soft dough. Transfer to a lightly floured surface and knead for 6–8 minutes, or until smooth. Put back in the bowl, cover with plastic wrap, and let rest for 20–25 minutes.

Divide the mixture into 8 pieces and flatten each one slightly. Cover with a kitchen towel and let rest for 10–15 minutes.

Put the dough on a lightly floured surface and roll each piece into a 9-inch disk. Brush the tops of the breads with melted butter and sprinkle over the nigella seeds. Put the breads on an oiled broiler pan and cook in batches, under a medium/high broiler for 1–2 minutes on each side, or until puffed up and lightly brown in spots. Wrap in a kitchen towel while you cook the rest. Serve warm with any curry.

extras

Chutney, relish, and pickles—all loyal curry companions and all essential in making a meal complete. To temper, enrich, or pep up, these extras are apt to fulfil any role. Even if all you want is to fill your plate with more finger-licking morsels, then **samosas (page 91)** are perfect extras. What's more, a bowl of **cilantro & mint chutney, cucumber & yogurt relish**, or **onion, cucumber & tomato relish (all page 88)** is so tempting that it's as good served as a dip when you've got the munchies, as it is as a bona fide accompaniment to a full-blown curry. In India, every household makes its own chutney and relish and stores them—it goes without saying that a homemade **mango chutney** or **carrot pickle (both page 93)** beats anything you can buy from a store so it's worth putting some jars together one weekend when you have an hour to spare. For a taste of the Tropics, nothing beats a **coconut chutney (page 92)**— snowy white and speckled with black mustard seeds and yellow split lentils. And let's not forget the ever-popular extras: pappadoms. Uncooked pappadoms are easy to find in supermarkets now, and just need to be fried or even popped in the microwave. But if you want to make more of them, try my **shrimp & pappadom rolls (page 90)**. There's no excuse not to bring a little of the inimitable Indian flair for flavor combinations into your home.

onion, cucumber & tomato relish

This is a finely chopped salad called "kachumber" and a common accompaniment in Indian meals. It is also great with pappadoms and bread.

1 red onion, finely chopped
1 cucumber, finely chopped
4 ripe tomatoes, finely chopped
a small handful of fresh cilantro leaves, finely chopped
1 red chile, seeded and finely chopped (optional)
freshly squeezed juice of 1 large lemon
⅓ cup roasted peanuts, roughly chopped

serves 4

Put the onion, cucumber, tomatoes, cilantro, and chile, if using, in a bowl and pour over the lemon juice. Season well, cover, and let stand for 10–15 minutes.

Before serving, stir well to mix and sprinkle over the chopped peanuts. This will keep in the fridge for up to 3 days.

cilantro & mint chutney

Quick and easy to prepare, this aromatic, fresh-tasting relish is great as a dip for snacks or to serve alongside broiled meat, chicken, or fish.

6 oz cilantro leaves, finely chopped
6 oz fresh mint leaves, finely chopped
freshly squeezed juice of 2 limes
2 green chiles, seeded and chopped
1 tablespoon finely grated fresh ginger
½ cup thick, Greek-style yogurt
1 teaspoon ground cumin
1 teaspoon mild chili powder
1 teaspoon sugar
sea salt

makes about 1¾ cups

Put the cilantro, mint, lime juice, chiles, ginger, yogurt, cumin, chili powder, and sugar in a small food processor and blitz until smooth (you might need to add a couple of tablespoons of water).

Season with sea salt and transfer to a bowl. Cover and chill until ready to use. This will keep in the fridge for up to 3 days.

cucumber & yogurt relish

"Raita" is a cool, yogurt-based relish which can be made from a variety of ingredients. This one is made with cucumber and mint— ideal for tempering a spicy meal.

1 small cucumber (approximately 6 inches), peeled and coarsely grated
1½ cups plain yogurt, whisked
5 tablespoons freshly chopped mint leaves
1–2 teaspoons cumin seeds, lightly toasted in a dry skillet
salt and freshly ground black pepper
mild or medium chili powder, to sprinkle (optional)

serves 4

Put the grated cucumber in a strainer and squeeze out as much liquid as you can. Transfer to a bowl with the yogurt and mint. Season well and chill until ready to serve. Sprinkle over the cumin seeds and chili powder, if using, just before serving. This will keep in the fridge for up to 3 days.

shrimp & pappadom rolls

Pappadoms are very thin dried disks made from a variety of different lentils. They are usually roasted or fried and served as a snack or a crispy accompaniment to a meal. Here they are stuffed with a spicy shrimp mixture and deep-fried. Uncooked pappadoms can now easily be found in most supermarkets. Serve with mixed, dressed salad greens, if you like.

Heat the sunflower oil in a large skillet and add the onion. Cook over gentle heat for 6–8 minutes or until softened. Add the garlic, ginger, cumin seeds, and curry powder and stir-fry for 1–2 minutes.

Add the shrimp and potatoes and stir well to mix. Season and stir in the cilantro and lime juice. Remove from the heat and set aside to cool.

Put the flour in a small bowl and stir in enough cold water to make a smooth, thick paste.

Soak the uncooked pappadoms in warm water for 3–4 minutes, or until just softened. Drain well, pat dry with paper towels, and put on a clean surface.

Spoon one-eighth of the shrimp mixture on to one side of a pappadom. Carefully roll it up, folding in the sides to enclose the filling. Apply a little flour paste around the edges to seal. Repeat with the remaining shrimp mixture and pappadoms to make the remaining rolls.

Fill a large saucepan one-third full with vegetable oil and heat to 310°F or until a piece of bread dropped in sizzles and lightly browns within 10 seconds. Carefully lower the stuffed rolls into the hot oil in batches and deep-fry for 2 minutes, or until golden and crisp. Drain thoroughly on paper towels and serve with mixed, dressed salad greens, if desired.

1 tablespoon sunflower oil
1 onion, finely chopped
1 teaspoon crushed garlic
1 teaspoon finely grated fresh ginger
2 teaspoons cumin seeds
1 tablespoon medium curry powder
5 oz raw shrimp, shelled, deveined, and roughly chopped
5 oz peeled and cooked potatoes, roughly chopped
¼ cup freshly chopped cilantro leaves
freshly squeezed juice of ½ lime
2 tablespoons all-purpose flour
8 medium-size, uncooked pappadoms
vegetable oil, for deep-frying
salt and freshly ground black pepper

serves 4

samosas

These popular golden stuffed packages can be filled with a variety of vegetable or meat mixtures. Here they are simply stuffed with spiced minced chicken.

Heat the sunflower oil in a skillet. Add the chicken, onion, and curry powder. Season and cook for about 10 minutes, uncovered, until the chicken is just cooked and the juices have evaporated from the pan. Add the potato and peas and mix well. Remove the pan from the heat and stir in the cilantro and mint. Let cool.

Lay the phyllo pastry dough out on a clean board and cut in half lengthwise, then in half once more widthwise, so that you have 4 rectangles from each whole sheet. Cover all the pieces of phyllo with a barely damp kitchen towel to prevent them from drying out. Take one piece of phyllo and lay it widthwise in front of you. Pile a spoonful of the chicken mixture on to the end closest to you. Fold the phyllo over the filling to form a triangle and continue to fold and enclose the filling until you have a triangular package. Brush the finishing edge with a little of the beaten egg to seal, then place on a baking sheet. Glaze the finished samosa all over with beaten egg and repeat the process until you have 20 samosas. These can be prepared earlier in the day up to this point and chilled in the fridge.

When ready to bake the samosas, preheat the oven to 425°F.

Bake the samosas in the preheated oven for 10–12 minutes, until golden brown in color.

2 tablespoons sunflower oil

10 oz ground chicken

1 onion, chopped

1 tablespoon medium curry powder

1 peeled and cooked potato, diced

⅓ cup frozen peas

¼ cup freshly chopped cilantro leaves

¼ cup freshly chopped mint leaves

5 sheets of phyllo pastry dough, each 10 x 20 inches, thawed if frozen

1 egg, beaten

salt and freshly ground black pepper

makes 20

coconut chutney

This is made with freshly grated coconut, however you could use about 1 cup desiccated coconut instead—just soak in hot water for 20–30 minutes, then drain well and use as below.

2 teaspoons dried yellow split lentils
1 cup freshly grated coconut
2 green chiles, seeded and finely chopped
1 teaspoon sea salt
2 tablespoons sunflower oil
2 teaspoons black mustard seeds
6–8 fresh curry leaves
1 dried red chile
1 teaspoon tamarind paste

serves 4

Rinse the lentils until the water runs clear. Drain, place in a deep bowl, and cover with cold water. Let soak for 2–3 hours. Rinse the lentils, drain, and set aside.

Put the coconut, green chiles, and salt in a food processor and blend to a fine paste (you might need to add a couple of tablespoons of water). Transfer to a bowl.

Heat the sunflower oil in a small skillet and add the mustard seeds and reserved lentils. Cook over gentle heat and when the mustard seeds start to pop, add the curry leaves and dried chile and stir-fry for 1 minute.

Add the spice paste and tamarind paste to the skillet, stir well to mix, and transfer to a bowl.

mango chutney

This lightly spiced, sweet chutney provides a lovely contrast to a spicy meal and is perhaps one of the best known and loved Indian chutneys.

1 tablespoon sunflower oil
1 teaspoon finely grated fresh ginger
2 garlic cloves, crushed
5 cloves
1 star anise
2 cassia barks or cinnamon sticks
5 black peppercorns
1–2 tablespoons nigella seeds
½ teaspoon mild or medium chili powder
1¾ lb ripe but firm mango flesh, roughly chopped
1⅔ cups white wine vinegar
1⅓ cups sugar
sea salt

1–3 sterilized jam jars (see page 4)

makes about 2 cups

Heat the sunflower oil in a saucepan over medium heat. Add the ginger, garlic, cloves, star anise, cassia, peppercorns, nigella seeds, and chili powder and stir-fry for 1–2 minutes. Add the mango, vinegar, and sugar and bring to a boil. Reduce the heat to low and cook for 45 minutes, or until the mixture is jam-like.

Season with sea salt to taste and pour into the hot sterilized jars. Seal and let cool before storing in the fridge for up to 2 months.

carrot pickle

Crunchy, spicy and full of zing, this carrot pickle will perk up even the simplest meal.

1 lb carrots, cut into 2-inch matchsticks
6½ oz small red shallots, peeled
6–8 green chiles
⅔ cup white wine vinegar
½ teaspoon ground turmeric
sea salt

pickling paste
⅔ cup white wine vinegar
4 garlic cloves, crushed
2 teaspoons finely grated fresh ginger
1 tablespoon black mustard seeds
2 teaspoons mild or medium chili powder
1 tablespoon sugar

1–3 sterilized jam jars (see page 4)

makes about 3 cups

Put the carrots, shallots, chiles, vinegar, and turmeric in a saucepan with 1¼ cups water and season with sea salt. Bring to a boil and cook for 3–4 minutes. Drain and set aside.

To make the pickling paste, put the vinegar, garlic, ginger, mustard seeds, chili powder, and sugar in a small food processor and blend until fairly smooth. Season with sea salt and transfer to a mixing bowl. Add the drained vegetable mixture and toss to coat evenly. Transfer to the hot sterilized jars. Seal and store in a cool, dark place for 2 weeks before eating. Store in the fridge after opening and eat within 2 months.

websites & mail order

www.igourmet.com
Tel: 1 877 446 8763
A trusted source for paneer, the traditional cheese used in Indian cooking.

Indian Foods Co
www.indianfoodsco.com
Tel: 1 866 416 4165
If you're searching for organic Indian herbs, spices, and teas, check out this comprehensive supplier. Explore the site for tastes from other curry-eating countries too. You'll find Thai chiles and curry pastes.

www.iShopIndian.com
A large variety of Indian foods and cookware plus music and movies.

Kalustyan's
www.kalustyans.com
123 Lexington Avenue
New York, NY 10016
Tel: 800 352 3451
For coconut cream, pappadams, chapatti flour (atta), dals, ghee, khus flavoring, spices, and premium Indian, Pakistani, and Thai rices, go to Kalustyan's.

Kitazawa Seed Co.
www.kitazawaseed.com
Tel: 510 595 1188
Can't find pea eggplants? Grow your own. Kitazawa Seed Company in Oakland, California is the oldest seed company in America specializing in Asian seeds.

Penzeys Spices
www.penzeys.com
Tel: 800 741 7787
For dried chiles, ground and whole spices including Kashmir "Mogra Cream" saffron, as well as a fine selection of fabulous curry powder blends, go to their website or browse the shelves of one of three dozen Penzeys Spices emporiums nationwide.

For useful kitchen equipment, woks, mortars and pestles, etc., check out these sites:

Chef's Catalog
www.chefscatalog.com
Tel: 800 338 3232

Crate & Barrel
www.crateandbarrel.com
Tel: 800 967 6696

Sur la Table
www.surlatable.com
Tel: 800 243 0852

Williams-Sonoma
www.williams-sonoma.com
Tel: 877 812 6235

index

conversion charts

Weights and measures have been rounded up or down slightly to make measuring easier.

Volume equivalents:

American	Metric	Imperial
1 teaspoon	5 ml	
1 tablespoon	15 ml	
¼ cup	60 ml	2 fl oz
⅓ cup	75 ml	2½ fl oz
½ cup	125 ml	4 fl oz
⅔ cup	150 ml	5 fl oz (¼ pint)
¾ cup	175 ml	6 fl oz
1 cup	250 ml	8 fl oz

Weight equivalents: **Measurements:**

Imperial	Metric	Inches	Cm
1 oz	25 g	¼ inch	5 mm
2 oz	50 g	½ inch	1 cm
3 oz	75 g	¾ inch	1.5 cm
4 oz	125 g	1 inch	2.5 cm
5 oz	150 g	2 inches	5 cm
6 oz	175 g	3 inches	7 cm
7 oz	200 g	4 inches	10 cm
8 oz (½ lb)	250 g	5 inches	12 cm
9 oz	275 g	6 inches	15 cm
10 oz	300 g	7 inches	18 cm
11 oz	325 g	8 inches	20 cm
12 oz	375 g	9 inches	23 cm
13 oz	400 g	10 inches	25 cm
14 oz	425 g	11 inches	28 cm
15 oz	475 g	12 inches	30 cm
16 oz (1 lb)	500 g		
2 lb	1 kg		

Oven temperatures:

110°C	(225°F)	Gas ¼
120°C	(250°F)	Gas ½
140°C	(275°F)	Gas 1
150°C	(300°F)	Gas 2
160°C	(325°F)	Gas 3
180°C	(350°F)	Gas 4
190°C	(375°F)	Gas 5
200°C	(400°F)	Gas 6
220°C	(425°F)	Gas 7
230°C	(450°F)	Gas 8
240°C	(475°F)	Gas 9